The GAMBOLS

BOOK Nº 34

by Dobs +
Barry Appleby

£ 1.50

MIGGY AND FLIVVER CAN ALWAYS THINK UP
SOME NEW WAY TO BE NAUGHTY

GAYE IS A REAL
'SOFTY' WHEN
IT COMES TO
LOOKING AFTER
'GRASS-WIDOWERS'

DO YOU
REMEMBER
WHEN......?

WE RECEIVE A LOT OF LETTERS FROM READERS TELLING US THAT THE GAMBOLS ADVENTURES ARE EXACTLY WHAT HAPPENS TO THEM—ONE LADY EVEN ACCUSED US OF HAVING A PERISCOPE IN THEIR HOUSE TO SPY ON THEM

"You have been chosen for a very special gift — just keep these lucky numbers and watch for the postman and send for....etc"

Oh dear — I suppose this sort of advertising pays or they wouldn't do it would they?

HALF·AN·HOUR·LATER

NO SOONER DOES A FASHION BECOME "ALL THE RAGE" THAN THEY INTRODUCE SOMETHING DIFFERENT

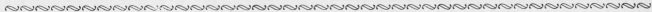

IT'S A **LOVELY** COLOUR

BUT A TRIFLE **TOO** PALE

A LITTLE LONG IN THE BACK

A BEAUTIFUL FIT

THE NECKLINE IS **VERY** CHIC

ER..YES — BUT I WOULD NEVER **DARE** TO LEAN FORWARD — WHAT DO YOU THINK GEORGE?

I'D RATHER NOT GET INVOLVED

29/41

IT'S NICE TO HAVE SOMETHING NEW TO WEAR

AND BE IN THE HEIGHT OF FASHION AGAIN

...FOR FIVE MINUTES

3090

DO YOU KNOW THAT MORE PEOPLE ACTIVELY TAKE PART IN FISHING THAN IN ANY OTHER SPORT?

GAYE SAYS THAT GEORGE ONLY NEEDS TO **SEE** A SET OF PLANS TO BECOME DIRTY

HERE ARE A FEW OF OUR BIGGER
CARTOONS WHICH YOU MAY NOT
HAVE SEEN

942

THAT SHOULD BE ENOUGH

NOW THE OTHER FRONT ONE

THE REAR TYRES NEED TWO POUNDS MORE THAN THE FRONT

PHEW! THANK GOODNESS THAT'S FINISHED

DID YOU REMEMBER THE SPARE WHEEL, DEAR?

912

841

893

892

EXCUSE ME — BUT HAVE YOU SEEN MY LITTLE DOGGIE?

885

WELL, THIS MORNING I HAD COFFEE WITH BRITT EKLAND – THEN LUNCH WITH ROCK HUDSON – THE AFTERNOON AT THE BEAUTY PARLOUR

FOLLOWED BY COCKTAILS WITH ELIZABETH TAYLOR AND HERE I AM

WHAT **DO** YOU THINK I'VE BEEN DOING WITH MYSELF ALL DAY?

898

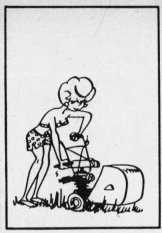

SOMETIMES I DON'T THINK YOU'LL **EVER** GET THE HANG OF IT

896

886

913

936

951

899

908

THE BEST PART ABOUT HOLIDAYS
IS THE PLANNING

GEORGE
DOESN'T LIKE
GAYE'S
SLIMMING
DIETS AT ALL

GAYE HAS
BECOME QUITE
USED TO
READING THE
OUTSIDE OF
THE NEWSPAPER
AT BREAKFAST

3059

CHILDREN COPY GROWN UPS BUT THEY DON'T ALWAYS COPY THE GOOD THINGS

SOME PEOPLE
DON'T SEEM TO
CARE HOW THEY
SPREAD THEIR
COLDS

WELL, HOW ELSE DO I REPAIR IT WITHOUT GETTING MY CLOTHES WET?

© 1984 Dobs + Barry Appleby 2926

A TINT, MADAM?

NO THANK YOU — A WASTE OF MONEY

A FACIAL?

SOME PERFUME?

NO THANK YOU

I PREFER TO SMELL CLEAN

NOW I KNOW WHY HER HUSBAND RAN OFF WITH HIS SECRETARY

© 1984 Dobs + Barry Appleby 2923

IT'S LOVELY TO BE ABLE TO SPEND MONEY YOU HAVEN'T GOT BY USING A CREDIT CARD .... UNTIL THE BILL ARRIVES!

GEORGE — HAVE YOU SEEN MY CREDIT CARD ANYWHERE?

©1985 Dobson Barry Appleby

3182

...AND ONCE AGAIN IT'S CHRISTMAS

AND THIS IS THE END OF ANOTHER GAMBOLS ANNUAL
— WE'LL BE IN THE USUAL PLACE WAITING TO MEET
YOU AGAIN TO·MORROW MORNING — DON'T FORGET —
THE DAILY EXPRESS AND THE SUNDAY EXPRESS

©1985 Dobs + Barry Appleby

Published by Express Newspapers Limited, Fleet Street, London, EC4P 4JT, and printed by Purnell and Sons (Book Production) Ltd., Paulton, Bristol.